THE WEAPONS ENCYCLOPÆDIA
TANK AIRCRAFT AFV SHIP ARTILLERY VEHICLES SECRET WEAPON

TWE-020 ENG

SEMOVENTI 75-34/46, 105/25, 90/53 & 149/40

THE WEAPONS ENCYCLOPAEDIA

EDITORIAL STAFF
Luca Cristini, Paolo Crippa.

ACADEMIC STAFF
Enrico Acerbi, Massimiliano Afiero, Aldo Antonicelli, Ruggero Calò, Luigi Carretta, Flavio Chistè, Anna Cristini, Carlo Cucut, Salvo Fagone, Enrico Finazzer, Arturo Giusti, Björn Huber, Andrea Lombardi, Aymeric Lopez, Marco Lucchetti, Gabriele Malavoglia, Luigi Manes, Giovanni Maressi, Francesco Mattesini, Daniele Notaro, Péter Mujzer, Federico Peirani, Alberto Peruffo, Maurizio Raggi, Andrea Alberto Tallillo, Antonio Tallillo, Massimo Zorza.

PUBLISHED BY
Luca Cristini Editore (Soldiershop), via Orio, 35/4 - 24050 Zanica (BG) ITALY.

DISTRIBUTION BY
Soldiershop - www.soldiershop.com, Amazon, Ingram Spark, Berliner Zinnfigurem (D), LaFeltrinelli, Mondadori, Libera Editorial (Spain), Google book (eBook), Kobo, (eBoook), Apple Book (eBook).

PUBLISHING'S NOTES
None of unpublished images or text of our book may be reproduced in any format without the expressed written permission of Luca Cristini Editore (already Soldiershop.com) when not indicate as marked with license creative commons 3.0 or 4.0. Luca Cristini Editore has made every reasonable effort to locate, contact and acknowledge rights holders and to correctly apply terms and conditions to Content. Every effort has been made to trace the copyright of all the photographs. If there are unintentional omissions, please contact the publisher in writing at: info@soldiershop.com, who will correct all subsequent editions.

LICENSES COMMONS
This book may utilize part of material marked with license creative commons 3.0 or 4.0 (CC BY 4.0), (CC BY-ND 4.0), (CC BY-SA 4.0) or (CC0 1.0). We give appropriate attribution credit and indicate if change were made in the acknowledgments field. Our WTW books series utilize only fonts licensed under the SIL Open Font License or other free use license.

CONTRIBUTORS OF THIS VOLUME & ACKNOWLEDGEMENTS
Ringraziamo i principali collaboratori di questo numero: I profili dei carri sono tutti dell'autore. Le colorazioni delle foto sono di Anna Cristini. Ringraziamenti particolari a istituzioni nazionali e/o private quali: Stato Maggiore dell'esercito, Archivio di Stato, Bundesarchiv, Nara, Library of Congress, Wikipedia, USAF, Signal magazine, Cronache di guerra, Fronte di guerra, IWM, Australian War Museum, ecc. A P.Crippa, A.Lopez, L.Manes, C.Cucut, archivi Tallillo. Model Victoria (www.modelvictoria.it) ecc. per avere messo a disposizione immagini o altro dei loro archivi.

For a complete list of Soldiershop titles, or for every information please contact us on our website: www.soldiershop.com or www.cristinieditore.com. E-mail: info@soldiershop.com. Keep up to date on Facebook https://www.facebook.com/soldiershop.publishing

Title: **ITALIAN SEMOVENTI - VOL. 2: 75/34-75/46-105/25-90/53-149/40** Code.: **TWE-020 EN**
Series by L. S. Cristini
ISBN code: 979125589-0782. First edition March 2024
THE WEAPONS ENCYCLOPAEDIA (SOLDIERSHOP) is a trademark of Luca Cristini Editore

THE WEAPONS ENCYCLOPÆDIA
TANK AIRCRAFT AFV SHIP ARTILLERY VEHICLES SECRET WEAPON

ITALIAN SEMOVENTI VOL. 2
75/34-75/46-105/25 90/53-149/40

LUCA STEFANO CRISTINI

BOOK SERIES FOR MODELERS & COLLECTORS

CONTENTS

Introduction .... Pag. 5
Semovente 75/34 .... Pag. 7
    Data sheet 75/34 e 46 .... Pag. 9
Semovente 75/46 .... Pag. 17
Semovente 105/25 .... Pag. 27
    Data sheet .... Pag. 36
Semovente 90/53 .... Pag. 37
Semovente 149/40 .... Pag. 47
    Data sheet 90/53 e 149/40 .... Pag. 50
Operational use .... Pag. 53
Camouflage and distinguish marks .... Pag. 55
Bibliography .... Pag. 58

▲ One of the first images of the prototype of the self-propelled 75/34 in the courtyard of the Ansaldo-Fossati workshops in Sestri Ponente on 26 February 1943. State Archives.

INTRODUCTION

This is the second and final book on the self-propelled vehicles of the Italian military forces up to 1945. In the first volume we dealt with the 75/18 self-propelled vehicle, and very partially with the 75/34. Other Italian 'light' self-propelled vehicles we dealt with in the two volumes on light tanks: the CV33 L3 and the L6 40. Here we will complete the later and more modern models in more detail: the self-propelled 75/34, 75/46, 105/25, 90/53 and the 149/40. The entire family of Italian tank fighters were designed to provide support for all our armoured forces, which were often unable to counter enemy vehicles.

During the Second World War, our self-propelled vehicles, especially those of the second generation discussed in this volume, but also the 75/18, were able to fight on an equal footing against almost all enemy armoured vehicles. As a demonstration of the quality of the vehicles, it must be remembered that even the Wehrmacht, which was usually less than tender in its 'unofficial' judgments of Italian vehicles, found the self-propelled vehicles to be very well-built, so much so that after 8 September, they were the Italian vehicles that it used the most. The serious and full-bodied reasons for the presence of these heavy vehicles referred to the need for the Italian army to have at its disposal armoured vehicles capable of opposing American, British and Russian ones.

▲ An Italian 75/34 self-propelled vehicle, already in German hands, has just been captured by British soldiers of the 78th Infantry Division who are examining the vehicle. The British have also already erased the German *balkenkreuz* and put the battleaxe badge of their division in its place. Italy, May 1944.

SEMOVENTE 75/34 M42 M CESANO DI ROMA, ITALY, SEPTEMBER 1943

▲ Semovente M42 75-34 belonging to the CXXXV Battaglione Controcarri of the 135th Armoured Division Ariete II. Cesano di Roma, September 1943.

SEMOVENTE 75-34

INTRODUCTION

We have already partly presented the 75/34 self-propelled gun in a few lines in the first volume dedicated to Italian self-propelled guns. The vehicle, an evolution of the more famous and widespread 75/18, was also a self-propelled assault gun (SPG) produced by Fiat-Ansaldo for the Regio Esercito. The main model of this self-propelled gun was the M42 M, while a few examples of the M43 model were produced towards the end of the war. After the armistice and the subsequent start of the Republican adventure in northern Italy, this vehicle was also adopted, albeit in rather low numbers, by the R.S.I.

DEVELOPMENT

The Regio Esercito had already adopted two self-propelled assault tanks in 1940: the 47/32 L40 self-propelled tank and the 75/18 M41 self-propelled tank for accompanying infantry and as tank destroyers. The latter in particular proved to be the only Italian armoured tank capable of holding its own against the British tanks. Realizing that the 75/18 howitzer was no longer an optimal choice, in June 1941 the Regio Esercito's top management requested an even more powerful self-propelled vehicle from Ansaldo, to which the company responded by proposing the installation of the 75/32 Mod. 1937 gun on the hull of the M41 self-propelled vehicle, itself derived from the M14/41 medium tank. However, this solution did not satisfy the army, which in October 1942 ordered the company's engineers to install the 75/34 Mod. S.F. piece on the hull of the M42 self-propelled vehicle. This second variant satisfied the General Staff and on 29 April 1943 the 'M42 M (modified) 75/34 self-propelled vehicle' was officially adopted and 280 units were ordered. The first vehicles entered service in May. Before the armistice, just over 90 units were produced, which went to equip the following army departments:

▲ In the autumn of 1944, many vehicles of the 'San Giusto' received a very complex camouflage, made of a dense network of brown and green spots on a sandy yellow background, such as this 75/34 (Viziano) self-propelled vehicle.

▲ A 75/34 M42M self-propelled vehicle outside the Ansaldo-Fossati plant in Sestri Ponente. It was a production vehicle assembled on 26 March 1943. Source: *Gli Autoveicoli da Combattimento dell'Esercito Italiano*.

▼ Rare wartime remnant of self-propelled 75/34 preserved in Messina at the Carristi Memorial.

- The 19th 'M' Tank Battalion of the 1st 'M' Armoured Division: based on 2 self-propelled batteries and 1 M15/42 tank company; each battery was equipped with a Command Self-Propelled Tank and three out of four sections;
- The XXX Counter-Tank Battalion of the 30th 'Sabauda' Infantry Division with 2 companies;
- The CXXXV Counter-Tank Battalion of the 135th Armoured Division 'Aries II' out of 3 companies;
- The 31st Tank Infantry Regiment and the 'Alexandria Cavalry' Regiment (14th).

After the armistice, the National Republican Army assigned some of them to the 'San Giusto' armoured squadron group. During the same period, the Wehrmacht also employed 80 newly produced and 36 captured from the Italians, renaming the vehicle StuG M42 mit 75/34 (851) (i). The vehicle was assigned to one company from each Panzerjäger Abteilung (tank fighter battalion) of many Heer divisions and some Luftwaffe Fallschirmjäger units in Italy.

■ TECHNICAL FEATURES

The layout of the new self-propelled vehicle echoes that of its 75/18 predecessors. The M42 hull derives from the M15/42 wagon, of which it retains the rolling train with semi-elliptical leaf spring suspension, the 192 hp Fiat-SPA 15TB petrol engine and the centre-rear section of the hull, without the turret. The front part of the vehicle consists of an armoured casemate made of bolted sheet metal, 50 mm thick on the front section. Unlike the 75/18, and due to the greater recoil of the new 75/34 gun, the armoured superstructure was lengthened by 11 cm at the front. An easily noticeable detail is the presence of a third bolt on top of the angled front armour plate. The conductor sits on the left and has a slot with an armoured hatch. In addition to the conductor, the casemate was occupied by the gunner leader, who had a periscope at his disposal for the (manual) aiming of the piece, and the servant, who eventually operated the Breda Mod. 38 machine gun, which could be installed on the top of the vehicle for anti-aircraft and short-range defence. The 75/34 Mod. S.F. cannon, designed for anti-tank fire, is always installed in the

DATA SHEET		
	75/34 M42/M43	75/46
Length	5040 mm	5100 mm
Width	2230 mm	2400 mm
Height	1850 mm	1750 mm
Start and end date	1942-1945	1944-1945
Total weight	15.300 kg	15.800 kg
Crew	3	3
Engine	Fiat SPA 15TB M42 petrol 8 V-cylinder, 11980 cm³	
Maximum speed	40 km/h on road 15 km/h off road	35 km/h on road 15 km/h off road
Autonomy	200 km on road 5 h off road	180 km on road 5 h off road
Total output	145 vehicles	11 to 18 vehicles
Armour thickness	14.5 to 50 mm	15 to 100 mm
Armament	75/34 Mod. S.F. gun with 46 shells. Secondary: 1 Breda Mod. 38 8 mm machine gun with 1104 rounds	Ansaldo 75/46 C.A. Mod. 1934 cannon with 42 shells. Secondary: 1 Breda Mod. 38 8 mm machine gun with 1000 rounds

▲ View of the 75/34 Model SF cannon mounted on trestles in the Ansaldo-Fossati factory. Source: fondazione-ansaldo.com. In the small picture: the Breda Model 1938 8 mm Medium machine gun, armoured version.

▼ An out-of-service 75/34 M42M self-propelled vehicle already in German service, and captured by the Allies with other equipment.

▲ Some Italian soldiers train to launch Breda model 1942 anti-tank hand grenades against a 75/34 M42 self-propelled 75/34 of the Cavalry Regiment 'Cavalleggeri di Alessandria'. State Archives.

centre of the casemate on a hemispherical mount, which allows a limited swing of 20° to the right and 20° to the left, with a lift of -12° to +22°. The internal ammunition racks were also upgraded to allow the loading of 45 rounds of 75 and about 1400 bullets for the machine guns. The increased interdiction capability of these new vehicles meant that both the Italians and Germans used the vehicle not so much in a support or self-propelled artillery function, but primarily as a tank fighter. Like the 75/18, the new vehicle also had armour entirely bolted to an inner frame. This arrangement was not optimal, and was of outdated design; however, it facilitated the replacement of an armour element should it need to be repaired. The armour was reinforced on the sides between 25 and 30mm while the front plate was 50mm thick. On the roof, on the other hand, it retained a thickness of 15mm, with little armouring on the bottom or floor. Only 6mm was obviously not enough to protect against mine explosions.

The engine of the Semovente M42M was the same, but slightly upgraded, engine in use on the earlier Semovente M42 75/18 and Tank M15/42. In addition to the increase in displacement, which improved the overall performance of the vehicle, the novelty was that the new engine ran on petrol instead of the diesel fuel that powered the engines of the M13/40 Tank, M14/41 Tank and the GSPs based on their hulls. The switch from diesel to petrol was due to the fact that Italian diesel reserves were almost completely exhausted by mid-1942. On the new 75/34 M42M self-propelled aircraft, thanks to the increased space in the engine compartment, the fuel tank capacity was increased to 367 litres in the main tanks, plus 40 litres in the reserve tank, making a total of 407 litres. Which in fact offered a greater operating range. The new FIAT engine also had a revamped gearbox with five forward gears and one reverse gear, one gear more than the previous vehicles. The suspension was the same as the 75/18, of the semi-elliptical leaf spring type. This type of suspension was obsolete and significantly slowed down the vehicle's ride. It was also very vulnerable to enemy fire or mines. The chassis of the new M42 had 26 cm wide tracks with 86 links per side, six more than the M13/40, M14/41 and 75/18 self-propelled tanks, due to the lengthening of the hull.

The vehicle's radio supply consisted of a Radio Phonic Transceiver Equipment 1 for Tank or RF1CA Receiver Equipment. This was a radiotelephone and radiotelegraph station with a power of 10 watts for both voice and telegraphy contained in a box measuring 35 x 20 x 24.6 cm and weighing about 18 kg. It was positioned on the left side of the superstructure, behind the driver's dashboard. Its operating frequency range was between 27 and 33.4 MHz. It had a range of about 8 km in voice mode and 12 km in telegraph

SEMOVENTE 75/34 M42 M CESANO DI ROMA, ITALY, SEPTEMBER 1943

▲ Semovente M42 75-34 belonging to the CXXXV Battaglione Controcarri of the 135th Armoured Division Ariete II. Cesano di Roma, September 1943.

▲ A 75/34 M42 self-propelled vehicle is loaded onto a French trailer 'La Buire'. The trailer is pulled by an M13/40 tank of the Gruppo Squadroni Armorati 'San Giusto'. The photograph was taken in the main street of Mariano del Friuli (Arena).

mode. However, these distances were drastically reduced when the self-propelled guns were in motion. The radio antenna mounted on this new self-propelled gun was of a new type. Previously, the old radio antennas were more complicated to move, lower etc. and could only be done from inside the vehicle. This new, much more practical one could be lowered manually at any angle.

ARMAMENT

The main weapon fitted to the 75/34 was the 75/34 Model SF [Sfera] cannon; it was derived directly from the 75/32 Model 1937 Long Range Cannon designed by the Royal Army Arsenal in Naples. As already mentioned, when the Army Staff requested a 75 mm long-barrelled cannon, Ansaldo responded with a totally new 75/36 cannon which, however, the military did not like it due to some of its deficiencies and it never went into production. The Naples Arsenal then proposed a 75/34 cannon obtained by mounting a new barrel, specially designed a few years earlier as a tank cannon. The solution from the Royal Army Arsenal in Naples was the one eventually chosen for the new self-propelled gun! It had 45 rounds available inside the casemate, together with almost 1,400 rounds of Breda ammunition.

The sight was mounted on the right side of the gun, and could be operated through a small opening hatch on the roof. It was then removed in those situations when it was not in use or when the hatch was closed. As secondary armament we always find the unfailing Breda Model 1938 8 mm Medium Machine Gun. On the 75/34 M42M Semovente the machine gun could be mounted on an anti-aircraft mount on the roof of the vehicle. When not deployed in an anti-aircraft role, the machine gun was stored on a mount on the right sponson of the combat compartment. Our self-propelled vehicle also adopted a complex system of fog grenades, introduced by copying a German system. However, this smoke curtain was only achieved at the rear of the tank, demonstrating the relative unreliability of the system.

SELF-PROPELLED 75/34 M42 M GERMANIC SERVICE, RIMINI, ITALY, SUMMER 1944

▲ Self-propelled M42 75-34 StuG M42 75-34 851(i) belonging to the 2nd Company 114th Panzerjäger Abteilung, Rimini, Italy, summer 1944.

CREW AND PRODUCTION

The crew of the vehicle consisted of three soldiers: the driver who was positioned on the left of the vehicle (to his right was the gun breech); the commander/gunner was positioned to the right of the gun breech and the loader/radio operator to the left, behind the driver. The duties assigned to the commander were to inspect the battlefield, identify targets, aim, open fire and, at the same time, give orders to the rest of the crew and listen to all messages transmitted by the radio operator. Many tasks were also assigned to the loader/serviceman, who in fact shared with the commander. In any case, the personnel on board the self-propelled vehicles were always chosen from among the best, while all the others were assigned to the medium or light tanks. These elite troops, so to speak, not only guaranteed better firing of the pieces assigned to them, but also significantly better maintenance of the self-propelled vehicle. Of all the 75/34 pieces produced, exact numbers are not available, due to the enormous confusion that arose at the turn of the armistice, but it is estimated that there were almost 150 examples, at least those delivered up to 8 September 1943. Of all these, the Germans immediately captured 36. The Germans themselves then restarted production of the vehicle and by the end of 1943, they obtained another 50. In 1944, Ansaldo then produced a further 25 75/34 self-propelled vehicles based on the hull of the Ansaldo 105/25 M.43. This differed from its predecessors in size, being wider and lower, and in its increased armour. These vehicles, renamed StuG M43 mit 75/34 851(i), were all used only by the Germans in northern Italy and the Balkans.

CONCLUSIONS

The 75/34 M42M self-propelled gun was one of the last Italian designs to be produced before the Armistice. Overall, it had interesting features, certainly starting with the weapon being able to take on many Allied medium tanks, something its predecessors had not been able to do. On the other hand, it had many sore points and shortcomings. It was built on an inadequate chassis, cramped inside and prone to frequent breakdowns, had an insufficient crew for the required performance and was forced to perform too many tasks.

▲ The M42M self-propelled 75/34 in German service (see profile on opposite page) with the new folding antenna. Note also the addition of four teeth on the front sprocket.

SELF-PROPELLED 75/34 M42 M GERMANIC SERVICE, ITALY OR BALKANS, 1944

▲ Self-propelled StuG M42 75-34 851(i) belonging to a German unit operating in Italy or the Balkans 1944.

SEMOVENTE 75-46

◼ INTRODUCTION

The M43 75/46 self-propelled gun, also known as the M42L (where L stood for long), being precisely 4 cm longer than the M42. It was the last self-propelled gun (SPG) produced by Italy during World War II. It was based on the earlier M43 self-propelled gun chassis, but featured a new spaced armour that offered better protection to the crew. It was developed by Italian companies at German request from late 1943. A total of 11 to 18 vehicles were produced, but most of the vehicles were delivered to the Germans, who deployed them on the Italian peninsula against the Allied forces in the final stages of World War II. It represented the most powerful Italian self-propelled tank fighter of the Second World War.

◼ DEVELOPMENT

The vehicle was derived from the self-propelled M43 'Bassotto', adopted by the Regio Esercito on 2 April 1943 and armed with the 105/25 howitzer, which we will discuss in the next chapter. Ansaldo's designer, engineer Giuseppe Rosini, developed the new tank destroyer by installing on the M43 hull the powerful 75/46 C.A. Mod. 1934 anti-aircraft gun, which proved to be an excellent anti-tank piece. The September armistice did not stop the programme, which was taken over by the German occupiers, with the production of 8 units in '43 and 3 in '44 renamed StuG M43 mit 75/46 852(i).

◼ TECHNICAL FEATURES

The M43 hull used for the self-propelled was derived from that of the M.15/42 tank, enlarged and lowered, with a redesigned front and welded instead of bolted side plates. Compared to the M43 hull of the 'Dachshund', of which it retained the general mechanical and performance characteristics, that of the M.75/46 self-propelled tank had reinforced armour, which was increased from 70 mm to 100 mm on the front, from 45 mm to 60 mm on the side plates and from 25 mm to 35 mm on the rear plates. The fighting compartment consisted of the bolted and welded fixed casemate, armed with the Ansaldo 75/46 C.A. Mod. 1934 cannon on a spherical mount, with a manual swing of 34° and a elevation of -12° to + 22°.

▲ Nice picture of the 75/46 M43 self-propelled vehicle placed outside the Ansaldo-Fossati factory. In this image, the 1944 Continental camouflage and the new Breda mount are clearly visible. Author's colouring.

The cannon had a penetration capacity (on vertical plates) ranging from 98 mm (at a range of 100 m) to 67 mm (at a range of 2400 m). The armament was complemented by a Breda Mod. 38 8 mm machine gun for close-range and anti-aircraft defence operated by the gunner/serviceman, while the radio servant/operator had a Magneti Marelli RF1 CA radio at his disposal for battery communications. The 74/46 gun was a really good artillery gun. It had a high initial muzzle velocity due to the use of a powerful propellant and the length of the barrel, a sustained rate of fire. The gun's breech had a system for switching from manual to semi-automatic opening, with a maximum rate of fire of 15 rounds per minute with a trained crew. Its initial velocity was 800 m/s and maximum range was 8,500 m in the anti-aircraft role (the role for which the piece was designed) and 13,000 m against land targets.

▪ GERMAN MODIFICATIONS

In fact, this modern self-propelled vehicle largely enjoyed the know-how of German engineering, as the Abteilung Waffen und Gerät beim Wehrkreiskommando 6 (Weapons and Equipment Department of Military District Headquarters No. 6 in Italy) took over the industrial reins of the Italian workshops, adopting construction criteria and/or variants that brought these vehicles up to the standards useful to the German army for which they were intended. It was they who greatly enhanced the armouring, increasing the total weight by more than 600 kg. The same mounted gun was also adapted to be able to fire German Pak 40 type ammunition. In addition to the new armour plates, other upgrades were made to the Italian self-propelled vehicles produced for the Germans. These included four larger teeth bolted to the outside of the gear wheel, intended to improve the efficiency of the gear wheel and its durability. Another modification requested

▲ The cannon mounted on the 75/46 was derived from the anti-aircraft piece of the same name, in the picture used by a German Flak company. Bundesarchiv. Author's colouring. In the small picture: another view of the 75/46 at Ansaldo.

SELF-PROPELLED 75/46 M42 T TANK DESTROYER, ITALY 1943

▲ Self-propelled M42T 75-46 tank version with 90° folded aerial, Italy 1943.

▲ An M43 self-propelled 75/46 used for the training of German Panzerjäger divisions in Italy. Visible are the Nebelkerzenabwurfvorrichtung mit Schutzmantel for the use of smoke grenades. Side: the radio system mounted on board the self-propelled vehicles (from the original logbook).

▼ 75/46 M43 self-propelled vehicle (left) next to a 105/25 M43 self-propelled vehicle without side skirts (right). Apart from the main armament and the added armour plates, the vehicles were identical.

SELF-PROPELLED 75/46 M42 T TANK DESTROYER, ITALY 1943

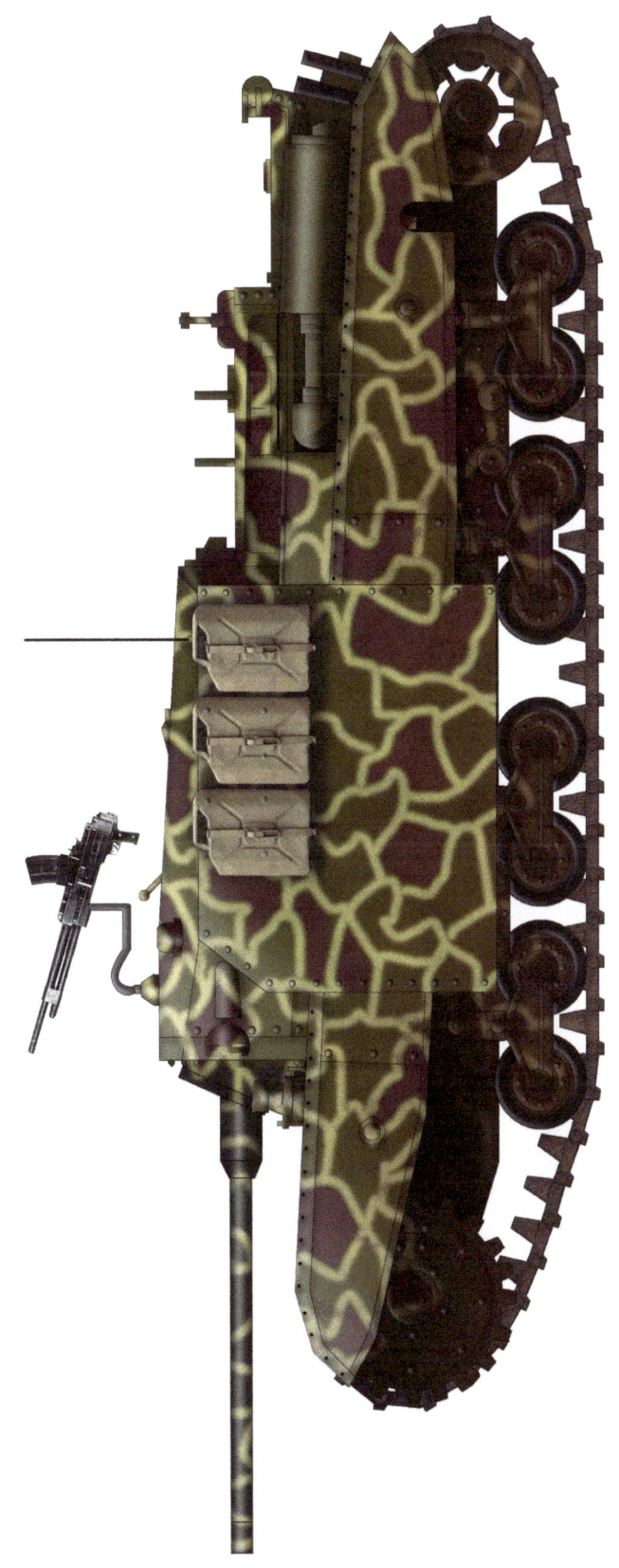

▲ Semovente M42 T from 75-46 version showing the special new type of support for the Breda on the roof of the vehicle and the reserve petrol cans. Italy 1943.

by the Germans was to replace the right roof hatch with one that could be opened in two parts for better ventilation of the fighting compartment.

A total of six 20-litre petrol canister racks were positioned on the sides of the vehicle, three on each armoured plate spaced on the sides, just as on other Italian self-propelled guns and tanks. It should be noted, however, that in post-1943 European, and thus German, use, on the M43 self-propelled 75/46 tanks, petrol canisters were no longer carried because they were no longer sent to North Africa, and there was no need to transport large quantities of fuel during operations in Italy or the Balkans, where the vehicle was risked. The interior of the casemate, radio equipment, engine and transmission, suspension etc. were essentially the same as the 75/34 M42M.

Final considerations on the cannon: the Germans and Ansaldo eventually decided to mount the 75/46 cannon on the M42T self-propelled vehicle, as repeatedly stated for its better anti-tank performance compared to the other Italian cannons at their disposal. However, this choice resulted in a very low production cadence due to technical problems, especially when compared to the cadence of all other self-propelled vehicles mounted on the same chassis. Consideration was therefore given to fitting the German Panzerabwehrkanone 40 as an alternative to the 75/46. The weight of the vehicle would not have increased much, only about 70 kg. Even before the armistice, Italy and Germany made arrangements to produce the famous PaK 40 (Italian nomenclature 75/43 Cannon Model 1940) locally. By 8 September, nothing had been done except to organise a few production lines. However, for reasons unknown, the Germans, once masters of the Italian industrial fabric, did not continue this project. However, after the armistice, OTO, thanks to the production lines mentioned above, produced some spare parts for the PaK 40 for the Germans until the end of the war. The secondary armament was always the Breda Model 1938 medium machine gun with an upper magazine without anti-aircraft sights. When not in use, it was stored

▲ British infantrymen engaged in combat during the Italian campaign, operating their mortars in the presence of a bulky 75/46 self-propelled carriage that had been put out of action. Interesting view of the openings.

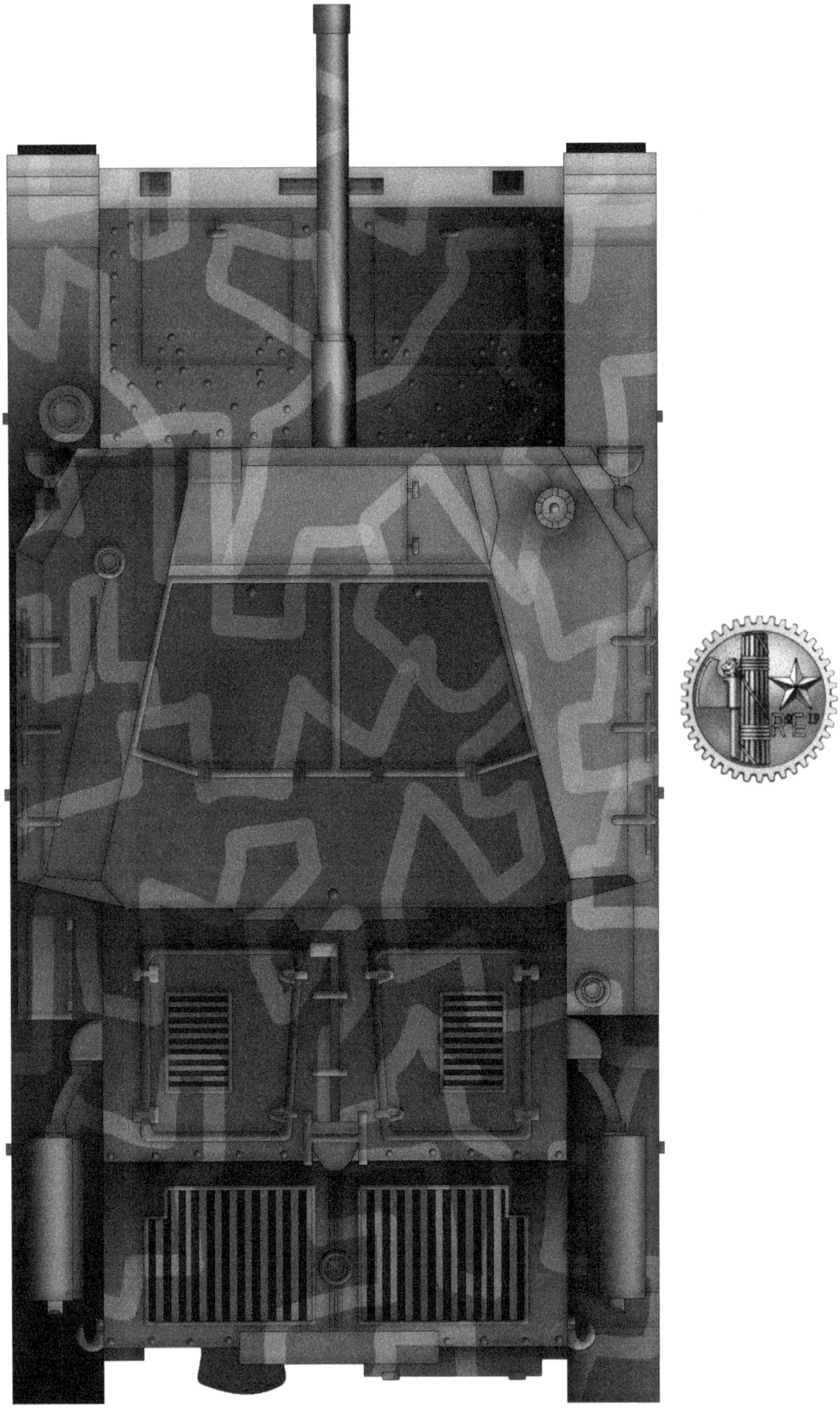

▲ View of the Italian 75/46 M43 self-propelled vehicle from above. On the right, the bronze or aluminium badge was placed on the front plate of the armoured vehicles from April 1936 to August 1943.

in the left sponsor of the self-propelled gun. The machine gun was mounted on a new anti-aircraft mount attached to a crowbar, which provided greater horizontal translation of the machine gun in the event of an air attack. After the Italian occupation by the Wermacht, all Bredas in gold possession were adapted for the 7.92 Mauser cartridges. As also stated in the file, the 75/46, like the previous self-propelled gun, was manned by a three-man crew. According to some unconfirmed sources, it seems that the Germans preferred to add a fourth crew member behind the gunner, who would load the weapon. Of course, adding a fourth crew member also meant drastically reducing the space inside the cramped combat compartment, which was already small for three crew members.

■ MINISKIRTS (OSTKETTEN)

An absolute novelty on this self-propelled vehicle was the fitting of so-called Ostketten, i.e. a kind of mini-skirt that, among other things, also had a protective function for the upper part of the tracks on both sides of the vehicle. These were probably additions decided by the Germans. Like the 105/35 M43 self-propelled vehicle, the 75/46 M43 was also equipped with a side miniskirt. These were only 4 mm thick and partially protected the sides of the vehicle. Their role was not so much to protect the self-propelled vehicle from anti-tank gun bullets or shaped charge ammunition, but to prevent shrapnel from damaging the suspension and track links. The side skirts had a cut-out at the rear to allow the crew to reach the track tension regulator without having to dismantle the mini-skirt. Three more small holes were also drilled to add lubricant to the idlers, again with the aim of not having to remove the side skirt.

▲ The M43 self-propelled 75/46 captured in a workshop in Milan by Italian partisans at the end of April 1945. Small photo: front sight for M43 75/46 self-propelled vehicle.

▲ View of the Italian 75/46 M43 self-propelled vehicle from front and rear.

SEMOVENTE 105/25 M43 'BASSOTTO' ITALY 1943

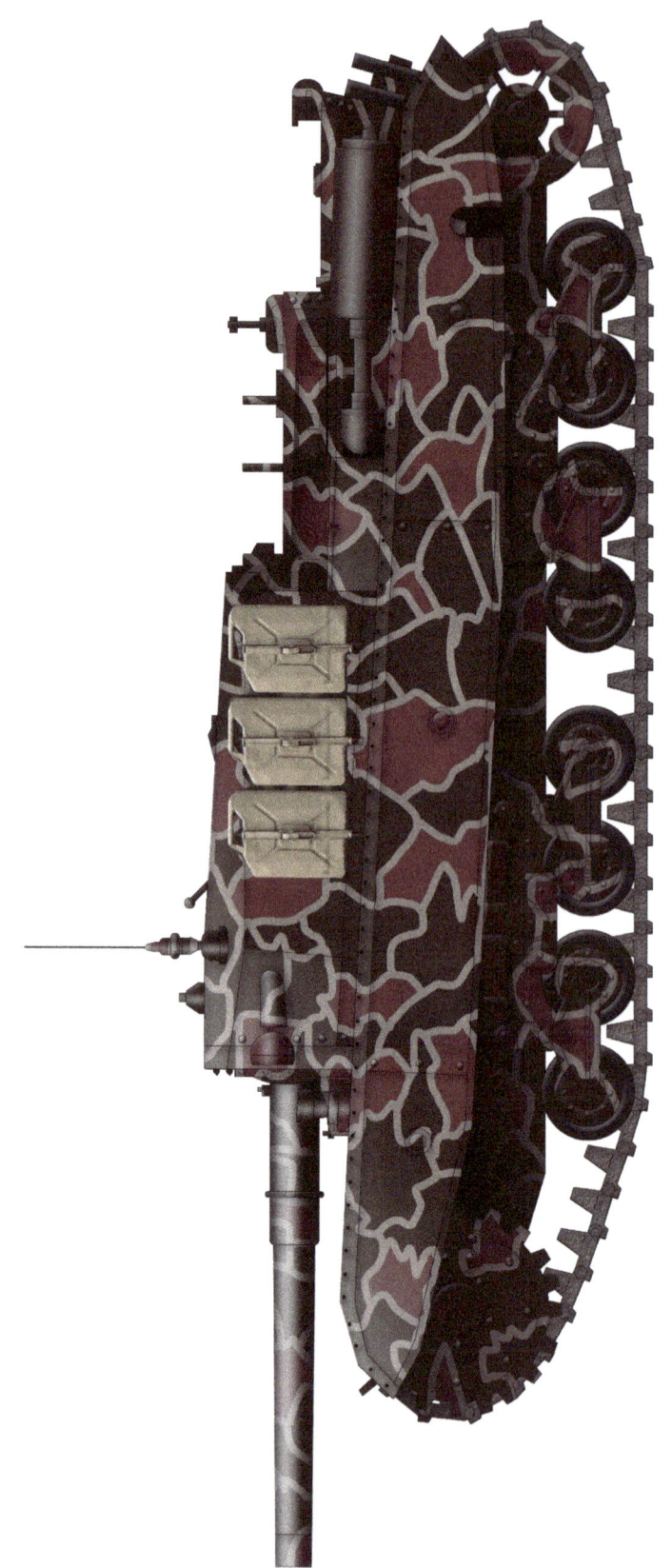

▲ Semovente M43 105/25 belonging to an R.E. unit in Italy, 1943

SEMOVENTE 105-25

INTRODUCTION

The Ansaldo 105/25 M.43, also known as the 105/25 self-propelled gun and commonly nicknamed the Dachshund ("bassotto" in Italian), was a valid Italian self-propelled gun used during World War II and designed by Fiat-Ansaldo, considered to be one of the most powerful self-propelled guns built by Italy in World War II. Also based on the design of the M42 75/18, it was little used by the forces of the Royal Army before the armistice, so that after the armistice signed at Cassibile and the occupation of central and northern Italy by the Germans, the self-propelled vehicles were captured and used by the German Army and the new Army of the RSI.

DEVELOPMENT

What has already been said about the self-propelled 75/34 and 46 also applies to the 105/25, which was created and put into production to overcome the objective shortcomings pointed out for the albeit good 75/18. So, in this case too, the development of a high-powered self-propelled vehicle was carried out during 1942 with a tender between Odero-Terni-Orlando (OTO) and FIAT-Ansaldo. The one proposed by Ansaldo was chosen because it was, among other things, more feasible and lighter, which meant it could be equipped with a less powerful petrol engine. This was a great advantage for the Italian Army, which had to replace diesel engines with petrol engines after 1942 due to limited resources. Testing of the prototype lasted several weeks. In the end, the Regio Esercito was very impressed by the firepower of the 105 mm cannon. Approved, an order followed for 130 vehicles divided into two batches, the first batch of 30 and a second of 100 self-propelled cannons. It was also officially renamed the 'Semovente FIAT-An-

▲ Fourteen M43 from 105/25, four M15/42 and a dozen M42M from 75/34 in the Ansaldo-Fossati factory in Genoa, ready for delivery to the Regio Esercito in July 1943.

▲ Officers of the DC Group of Self-Propelled Units pose in front of a brand new 105/25 M43 self-propelled vehicle that had just been delivered to the department at the Nettunia range in the late summer of 1943 (Pignato).

▼ A self-propelled 105/25 loaded onto a fast transport trailer to be transported to the operational area. State Archives. Author's colouring.

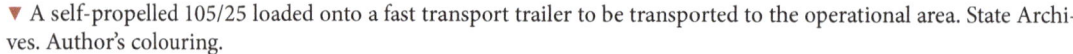

SEMOVENTE 105/25 M43 "BASSOTTO" SERVICE REGIO ESERCITO, ITALY 1943

▲ Semovente M43 da 105/25 belonging to an RE unit in Italy, 1943.

saldo su scafo M43 da 105/25', abbreviated to 'Semovente M43 da 105/25', but among its crews it became known by the nickname 'Dachshund' due to its lower and wider profile. Several others were added to the first order until there were around 800 in total. The events of September '43 nipped this ambition in the bud. However, in May of the same year, twelve examples were built and used in 1943 by the 135th Armoured Division 'Aries II'. Following the Italian surrender, the Germans, who considered the self-propelled 105/25s to be excellent vehicles, captured them and reopened the construction lines, building a further 91 examples, renamed StuG M43 mit 105/25 853(i) and using them against Anglo-American forces. At the turn of 1944-45, one example was also used by the RSI's 'Leoncello' Armoured Group near Brescia. The 105/25 gun was also posted in casemates in the defensive works of the Vallo Alpino.

■ TECHNICAL FEATURES

The Dachshund, following the general layout of its M42 predecessor, consisted of an M43 hull, i.e. the hull of an enlarged and lowered M15/42 tank, with a redesigned front and welded instead of bolted side plates. On the hull was a fixed casemate bolted and welded with an Ansaldo 105/25 howitzer, with a manual swing of 34° and elevation from -12° to + 22°. The armament was complemented by a Breda Mod. 38 8 mm machine gun for close-range and anti-aircraft defence operated by the tank leader/cannon fighter, while the servant/radio operator had a Magneti Marelli RF1 CA radio at his disposal for battery communications. The M42's hull was 14 cm longer than previous self-propelled aircraft. The new hull of the M43 (also known as the M42 'Long') was even longer, 4 cm longer than the M42, reaching a length of 5.10 m, 17 cm wider and 10 cm lower. All these modifications added up to a total vehicle weight of 15.8 combat-ready tonnes compared to the M42's 15 tonnes. This made the vehicle's silhouette more elusive and lower and also allowed the gun to be placed in the centre of the superstructure, instead of being moved to the right, as on the previous 75/18 chassis. The armour was both bolted to an inner frame and welded (a necessary improvement for Italian vehicles) and was finally thicker than Italian standards. The

▲ Interesting comparative view of a 75/18 M42 (left) and the 105/25 M43 prototype (right) at the Ansaldo-Fossati factory in Genoa. The wider and lower hull of the 'Dachshund' is evident.

SEMOVENTE 105/25 M43 'BASSOTTO' RSI SERVICE, ITALY, SUMMER 1944

▲ M43 self-propelled 105/25 mounted on M15/42 chassis belonging to the RSI's Leoncello armoured division, Italy 1944.

▲ A StuG M43 105/25 captured by the Germans. Photo taken a few days after the Armistice. Author's colouring.
▼ Souvenir photo of German soldiers standing on the roof of a self-propelled 105/25. Author's colouring.

hull armour was 50 mm at the top and 25 mm at the bottom. The superstructure had 70 mm thick armour at the front, 45 mm at the sides, while at the rear it was protected by a 35 mm thick plate. A plate of the same thickness protected the rear of the engine compartment. The roof and floor of the vehicle were 15 mm thick. New to the vehicle were the so-called Ostketten, i.e. side skirts divided into three parts. These were 4/5 mm thick. They partially protected the sides of the vehicle. The side skirts had a hole in the rear to allow the crew to reach the track tension regulator. The good armour reinforcement was partly rendered futile by the fact that the Italian industry was unable to supply good quality ballistic steel. As a result, although thick, the Italian armour was fragile compared to armour of equal thickness from other nations involved in the war. When an enemy bullet hit the Italian armour, it would often break or splinter even without being pierced, causing damage to the vehicle and often to the crew members, very often forcing the units to send the vehicle to specialist workshops to replace the damaged armour plates. The external bodywork had some new features. The most obvious was the longer and wider casemate than that of the 75/18.

On the roof, on the left side, was the radio antenna, which could now be folded down in a more practical manner, a fully rotatable periscope and an opening for the cannon. The commander was equipped with an optical sighting system manufactured by Ansaldo and weighing around 13 kg. On the rear and sides of the vehicle were a jack stand, storage compartments and other tools. On the sides of the casemate were two headlights for night operations. The engine compartment was equipped with grilles for cooling the engine. Behind them were the fuel tank cap and two grilles for cooling the radiator. At the rear were a spare wheel, a hole for the engine crank, the tow hook and a complex smoke grenade launcher system consisting of a grenade launcher and a smoke grenade rack for reloading the grenade launcher. Unfortunately, this only functioned at the rear of the vehicle and was also boring at the sides or front of the vehicle. On the sides of the rear area were mufflers covered by a steel shield to protect them from impact. On the sides of the vehicle were six racks, three per side, for 20-litre petrol cans, just like on other Italian self-propelled and armoured vehicles. This equipment was particularly designed for the African theatre where the canisters would increase the vehicle's autonomy. It should be noted, however, that in most cases, 105/25 M43 self-propelled vehicles did not carry jerry cans because fuel was not so difficult to obtain in Italy. For the suspension, we refer to the previous chapter on the self-propelled 75/46.

ARMAMENT

The main variation in all Italian self-propelled vehicles lies in the cannon. In this case, the main armament was a 105/25 howitzer (sometimes also called Mod. SF 'Sferico') produced by Ansaldo. It was developed on the basis of the 105/23 Mod. 1942 howitzer, which in turn was developed from an OTO-Melara howitzer as a prototype for divisional artillery together with the 105/40 Mod. 1938 howitzer. Unfortunately for the Italian Armed Forces, the new gun was tested and thus produced too late, thus having little effect on the state of the conflict. At least two prototypes of the 105/23 Mod. 1942 howitzer were produced. One, or perhaps more, were on a field mount and one on a spherical mount intended for the prototype of the 105/25 M43 self-propelled gun. The field version of the gun intended for the dachshund had a maximum range of 13 km and a range of 2,000-2,500 m with anti-tank ammunition. It had a practical rate of fire of 8 rounds per minute. Obviously, within the narrow combat compartment of the self-propelled gun, this cadence decreased dramatically. The weight of the weapon is not stated in the sources, it can be estimated at something less than a tonne together with its spherical mount. For reference, the 105/28 Mod. 1912 cannon, also produced by Ansaldo and of a similar type and ammunition, had a barrel length of 2.987 m (compared to 2.6 m for the 105/25) and weighed 850 kg. Due to the extension of the vehicle, the spherical cannon mount was placed centrally on the front plate. The cannon had a horizontal translation of 18° to the right and 18° to the left, as well as an elevation of +18° and a depression of -10°. As always, the secondary armament consisted of a Breda Mod. 38, the vehicle version of the Breda Mod. 37 medium machine gun used by the Italian infantry. The machine gun weighed 15.4 kg and was equipped for the Breda 8×59

RB cartridge. The Breda Mod. 38 had a theoretical rate of fire of 600 rounds per minute, which in practice dropped to about 350 rounds per minute. One of the advantages of this machine gun, besides its reliability, was its small size. In fact, the machine gun was only 89 cm long and took up little space once stored inside the vehicle. In addition to the Breda, the crew also had the official Carcano Mod. 91, or MAB 38 machine guns and 35 hand grenades for close defence against enemy infantry.

The engine, crew, radio system and division of the interior space of the self-propelled vehicle are similar to those already described in the other self-propelled vehicles in this volume.

▲ A StuG M43 105/25 captured by the Americans (left). On the right an M43 105/25 StuG captured by the Germans in Rome after the Armistice. Note the original Regio Esercito plate, RE 6453. Rome, March 1944.

▲ A photo of the 105/25 M43 self-propelled vehicle of the 'Leoncello' Group. The vehicle bears the battle name "TERREMOTO" on the front of the casemate and also seems to have a number plate, but it is impossible to tell if the latter has a numbering or if only the white rectangle, with no numbers, has been painted. On board the vehicle is Captain Zuccaro, who appears to be wearing a black beret. Several copies of this photograph were distributed to the Group's Carristi and the back bore a dedication from the commander similar to this one: 'For Domenico Noè in the certainty of his loyalty to the end! Captain Zuccaro P.d.C. 867 13.3 XXIII' (Arena archive).

SEMOVENTE 105/25 M43 'BASSOTTO' GERMAN SERVICE, ITALY, SUMMER 1944

▲ M42L/43 self-propelled vehicle on M42L hull (StuG M 43 105-25 853(i)) of 2nd Battery 914th Sturmgeschutz Brigade, Italy, summer 1944.

▲ A 105/25 made useless and then abandoned by its German crew is inspected by a British soldier. Clearly visible through the open hatch is the FIAT-SPA T15B engine.

DATA SHEET	
	Semovente 105/25 M43
Length	5100 mm
Width	2400 mm
Height	1750 mm
Start and end date	1943-1945
Total weight	15.800 kg
Crew	3
Engine	Fiat SPA 15TB M42 petrol 8-cylinder V-cylinder, 11980 cm³
Maximum speed	35 km/h on road 15 km/h off road
Autonomy	180 km on road 5 h off road
Total output	121 vehicles
Armour thickness	15mm, 45mm lateral to 70mm frontal
Armament	105/25 Ansaldo howitzer with 48 grenades. Secondary: 1 Breda Mod. 38 8mm machine gun with 864 rounds

SEMOVENTE 90/53

INTRODUCTION

The self-propelled 90/53 was an armoured artillery gun, also used as a tank destroyer, produced in Italy during the Second World War based on the idea of Colonel Sergio Berlese, an esteemed Italian designer and member of the Artillery Technical Service. The armament consisted of a 53-calibre (L/53) Mod. 1939 90/53 cannon. Between 30 and 48 examples were produced during 1942.

DEVELOPMENT

In the course of Operation Barbarossa, the powerful and innovative Soviet T-34 and KV-1 tanks appeared, equipped with armour and armament superior to the standards of the time. These proved to be a tough opponent even for the best-equipped German tanks, let alone the Italian armed forces.
The Italian Expeditionary Corps in Russia (CSIR), which arrived on the Eastern Front in July 1941, saw this enormous disadvantage first-hand. At first, the idea was therefore to use a gunship initially designed for anti-aircraft fire in a sort of new anti-tank function. Somehow emulating the success achieved by the Germans with their 88 mm Flak. The Italian General Staff then opted for the 90/53 90 mm anti-aircraft gun produced by Ansaldo. It had a performance similar to, and in some areas superior to, even the 88-mm Flak series. The design was based from the beginning on the hull of the M13/40 tank, then time was lost waiting to decide which gun tube to adopt. Finally, in December 1941, plans were ready for the new 90/53 Mod 39 Ansaldo cannon. The complete design was finalised in January 1942 and the first prototypes were set up and the first tests carried out. On 5 March of the same year, a working model was taken to firing tests at the special bench at the Ansaldo-Fossati factory in Sestri Ponente. Five months after these tests, the first six actual examples were assembled.

▲ Members of the Italian crew (the first on the left is Dino Landini) posing for souvenir photos probably after the 90/53 training in Nettuno, near Rome.

■ TECHNICAL FEATURES

The cannon was mounted on the hull of the M14/41, which was lengthened by 17 cm to better fit the weapon system and with the rear suspension shifted back, which was very important as it allowed the cannon position to be set significantly back. Among other things, this made it possible to greatly facilitate firing operations. An ideal solution was therefore achieved, with the only major drawback of not being able to obtain a casemate or a space suitable for the crew of the vehicle. So the servants had to travel in a separate vehicle. The actual crew on board the self-propelled vehicle therefore consisted only of the pilot and the tank leader. The gun carriage underwent several modifications to be adapted to the M14's hull: the cradle was redesigned in order to move the trunnions to a barycentric position, the balancers, the sub-barrel and related manoeuvring parts, and the shielding were removed. The swing covered an arc of 40° to the right and 40° to the left, while the elevation ranged from -5° to +24°. The piece proved to be an effective anti-tank weapon, capable of piercing even heavy Mk VIII Churchills with front armour more than 100 mm thick, provided the targets were less than 500 metres away. The main shortcoming of the vehicle was the lack of space in general, and not only for the crew, but also for ammunition: each self-propelled vehicle could therefore only carry eight grenades, the difference being that eighty-six were transported on an L6/40 light tank suitably modified as an ammunition carrier, which could also serve as a transport for the other two crew members. As a self-propelled artillery vehicle operating at a good distance from the front line, the vehicle maintained a modest armour plating: the hull was 30 mm thick at the front, 25 mm on the sides and rear, 15 mm for the roof and 6 mm on the bottom; the small superstructure also acting as a cape was 41 mm thick and sloping at 28° (sloping compared to vertical armour). Finally, the cannon shield was 30mm thick. Behind the shield were the two gunners with their seat positions aligned. The main defect of the 90/53 was due to the fact that it was designed for anti-aircraft fire only (unlike the German 88mm), and therefore lacked specific ammunition dedicated to anti-tank fire, and therefore operated with a generic armour-piercing projectile, which did not do justice to the (excellent) quality of the gun. It also lacked an EP (ready effect) projectile, i.e. the Italian equivalent of the hollow charge. Thus, al-

▲ Close-up of an M41M 90/53 self-propelled vehicle with the Regio Esercito 5824 licence plate.

SELF-PROPELLED 90/53 M41 ITALY, SEPTEMBER 1943

▲ Semovente M41M da 90/53 belonging to the CXXXV Battaglione controcarri 135a D.C.Ariete II Cesano di Roma, Italy, September 1943.

▲ Another view of an M41M 90/53 self-propelled vehicle of the Regio Esercito mimetic coloured.

▼ Rear view of the cuirass of the gun of the M41M 90/53.

SELF-PROPELLED 90/53 M41 ACTIVE IN SICILY, ITALY, JULY 1943

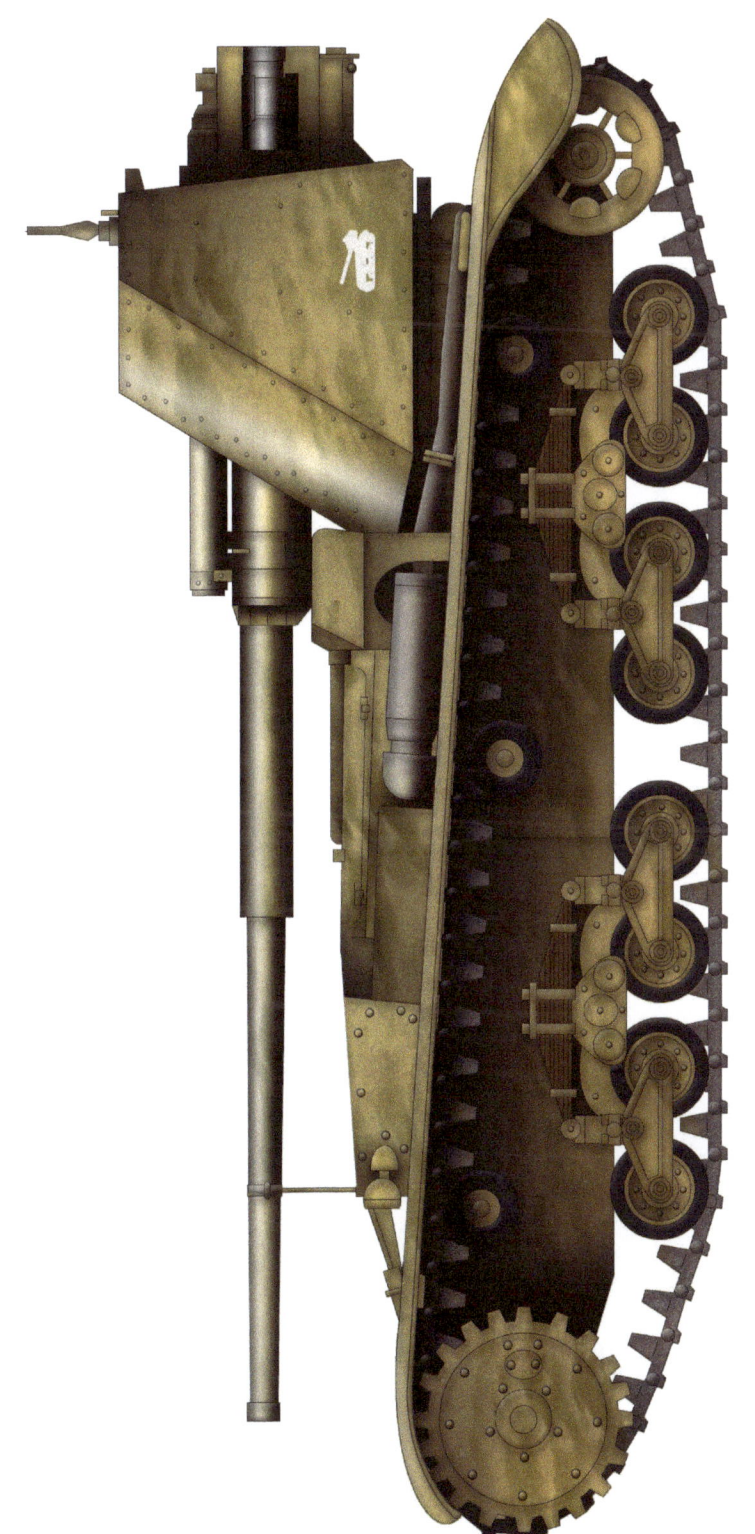

▲ M41M 90/53 self-propelled tank of the CLXIII Gruppo Controcarri Semoventi in Sicily sand-yellow camouflage version, Sicily, Italy, July 1943.

SEMOVENTI 75-34/46, 105/25, 90/53 & 149/40

▲ Semovente da 90/53 of the CLXIII Group abandoned by the Italians near Canicattì. Source: Sicily 1943. Author's colouring.

▼ The ammunition transport vehicle, made from the L6/40 converted from the Ansaldo-Fossati plant, towing a Viberti supplementary ammunition trailer. Source: Ansaldo.

SELF-PROPELLED 90/53 M41 GERMANIC SERVICE, ITALY 1943-1945

▲ M41M self-propelled 90/53 Beute Gepanzerte-Selbstfahrlafette of the 26th Panzer Division, Italy 1943-45.

SEMOVENTI 75-34/46, 105/25, 90/53 & 149/40

HYPOTHETICAL M41 SELF-PROPELLED AIRCRAFT 149/40, ITALY 1943

▲ Hypothetical study for the realisation of the 149/40 self-propelled vehicle on an M41 hull that was never built. Italy 1943.

though very powerful for the average Italian, the 90/53 was for many reasons a big missed opportunity. It missed its goal of becoming an outstanding weapon due to the above-mentioned shortcomings. Another serious shortcoming of the 90/53 self-propelled gun was the fact that long and laborious operations were required before opening fire; therefore, its use could only be envisaged in a static environment and not in mobile warfare conditions. For this reason, seeing these limitations, it was decided not to send it either to Africa or Russia where it would not be able to operate at its best. The light armouring and the open structure of the gun also did not protect the artillerymen from enemy infantry fire and even worse from attack by low-flying machine-gun aircraft. Finally, the need to share ammunition on one vehicle, typically the L6/40 tank transport version, and the gun exposed the entire gun-and-crew system to great reliability risks, which were well understood by the Italian armoured unit commanders once their superiors had already started to produce this self-propelled unit. In practice, for all these reasons, it was not recommended for use as an anti-tank gun (which was what they were trying to achieve), and consequently, doubts were also raised as a self-propelled support gun (the 90 mm was 'only' a direct-firing piece, not an indirect-firing piece like the 75/18, or direct-indirect like the 75/34 and 105/28, used by the other Italian self-propelled units). For this reason, despite the great need for modern tanks on all fronts, the use of this self-propelled unit was postponed and all but forgotten, being used only and with little success in Sicily during the Allied landings.

CONCLUSIONS

Many sources and several armoured vehicle enthusiasts consider the 90/53 M41M self-propelled gun to be a poorly designed self-propelled gun that, apart from the powerful main gun, had nothing exceptional about it. In addition to the shortcomings we have already pointed out, it must also be said that all the crews came from artillery regiments and had basic training in static artillery equipment or at best truck repair. They received only limited and too quick training on armoured vehicle repair at the Nettuno training school before being transferred to Sicily. Of the two theatres for which the vehicle was designed, the Russian one would not have been ideal, while perhaps the African front would have offered more opportunities for this type of weapon. Fundamentally, it remains that realised as a tank fighter, it never actually did so, due to what has been said and also to the very small number of vehicles produced.

▲ M41M 90/53 self-propelled aircraft at Ansaldo-Fossati. The white roundel on the roof of the superstructure was painted for aerial recognition. Source: Ansaldo.

SELF-PROPELLED 149/40 M42 PROTOTYPE, ITALY 1943

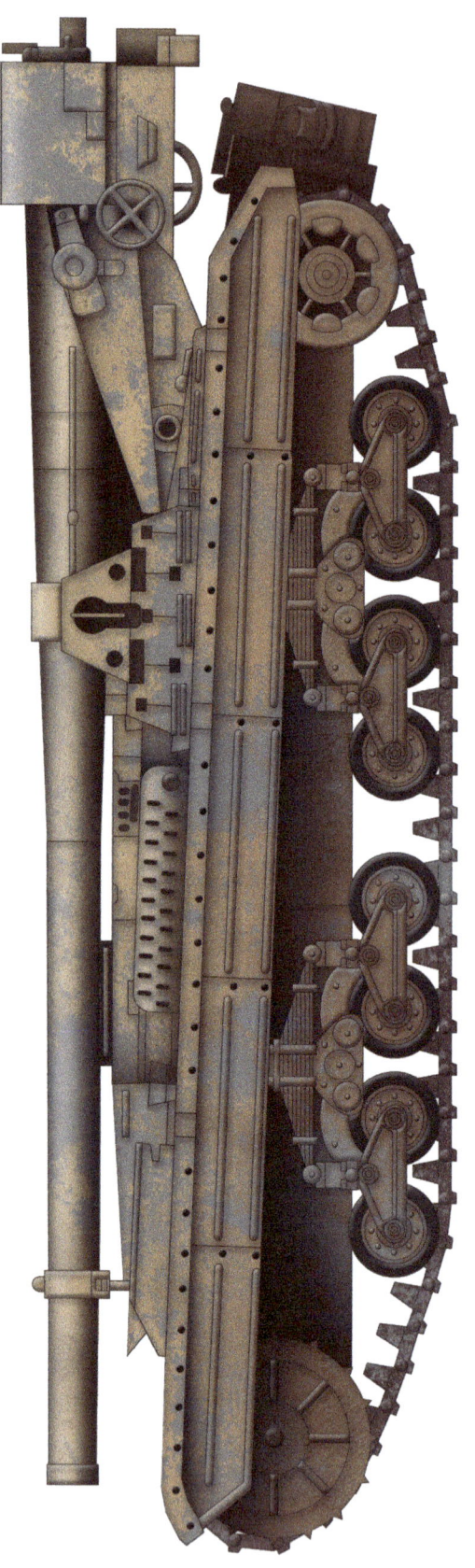

▲ Semovente 149/40 M42 prototype original camouflage version, Regio Esercito, Italy 1943.

SEMOVENTE 149/40

INTRODUCTION

The 149/40 self-propelled vehicle was an Italian prototype self-propelled vehicle powered by a 183.44 kW (246 hp) SPA engine and armed with a 149 mm artillery piece. It was a gun installation, the largest ever conceived for an Italian self-propelled vehicle!

DEVELOPMENT

Ansaldo, which produced the 149/40 mm Mod. 1935 field gun with mechanical drive, thought that a self-propelled version on a tracked hull might be a good idea and would be less expensive and more practical to use. In 1942, the management of the Artillery Works decided to proceed with the construction of a prototype to be submitted to the Royal Army. The hull was built from scratch, on which the 149 mm piece would be mounted at the rear, combined with the steering assembly type taken from the M15/42, with suspension taken from the P26/40 model suitably strengthened to withstand the weight of the gun. And finally to a powerful engine, the 246 hp SPA 228 petrol engine.

The design was started in April 1942 and the prototype was ready in August 1943, the same month it carried out some firing trials in Genoa. It was planned to produce 20 units by December 1943, but the particular political moment caused production to be abandoned.

So only the prototype remained. A few days after the firing trials, the prototype was requisitioned by the Germans, who re-designated it gepanzerte Selbstfahrlette M 43 mit 15 cm L/42 854(i). The 149/40 self-propelled gun was transferred by rail to Hillersleben in Germany, where it was later found by US troops and transferred to the United States of America to the Aberdeen Proving Ground in Harford County in the state of Maryland.

ARMAMENT

The armament coincides with the Ansaldo 149/40 Mod. 1935 howitzer alone. It had a maximum range of almost 22 km, with an initial speed of 800 m/s and a firing cadence of about one shot per minute as normal (equal to 60 shots per hour).

Battery firing was only possible with ground ploughshares, which, however, made an excellent impression both in terms of stability and the ability to operate on all types of terrain. In addition, compared to the 149/40 self-propelled piece, it had the advantage that it could be quickly put into position, required less manpower, was protected in its propulsion organs and weighed less (24 tonnes as opposed to 32 for the gun and two tractors for transport).

CREW

Like most information concerning this obscure vehicle, the number of men required to operate it effectively is unknown. Sources often mention that the vehicle had only two crew members, but this probably refers, as in the case of the relative 90/53, only to those who were stationed inside the vehicle. This would include the driver and probably the commander, but could also be any member of the crew. The rest of the crew would again presumably be transported in an auxiliary vehicle. Ideally, a fully tracked vehicle would be used in this role to keep up with the 149/40 M43 Self-Propelled Vehicle.

CONCLUSION

The M43 self-propelled 149/40, was certainly a rather interesting Italian vehicle with a modern concept for the times. It was designed and built with the intention of providing mobility for heavier weapons. Unfortunately, the notorious and serious Italian industrial situation, the lack of resources and the concomitant need for armoured vehicles of all types caused this project to be shelved.

▲ The only example of the self-propelled 149/40 is now housed in an open-air museum in the United States, at the US Army Ordnance Museum in Aberdeen.

▲ Beautiful view of the breech of the self-propelled preserved in the USA. Well maintained, it has received several non-original paint jobs over the years.

▼ The elevation of the self-propelled M43 149/40 gun was the same as the towed version, but the translation was slightly lower, at 53°. Source: Ansaldo Archives. Author's colouring.

SELF-PROPELLED 149/40 M42 PROTOTYPE, ITALY 1943

▲ Semovente 149/40 M42 original prototype Royal Army, Italy 1943.

DATA SHEET		
	M41 90/53	M43 149/40
Length	5210 mm	6500 mm
Width	2200 mm	3000 mm
Height	2150 mm	2000 mm
Start and end date	1942-1945	1943
Total weight	17.000 kg	24.000 kg
Crew	4	3
Engine	Fiat SPA 15TM 41 a benzina	8 cilindri a V. (90/53) Motore a benzina SPA 250 VV (149/490)
Maximum speed	25 km/h on road	35 km/h on the road
Autonomy	200 km on the road	180 km on the road
Total output	30 to 50	A prototype
Armour thickness	15 to 30 mm	15 to 25 mm
Armament	90/53 cannon Mod. 1939	Ansaldo 149/40 Mod. 1935 cannon

▲ Interesting photo of the 149/40 M43 self-propelled prototype, captured by the Allies in Germany, and then taken to this military depot near Paris in 1944, before ending up in the USA. Author's colouring.

SEMOVENTE 149/40 M42 GERMAN SERVICE, 1943-1945

▲ Semovente 149/40 M42 in German service camouflage version, 1943-1945.

▲ An artilleryman shows a 90/53 bullet. Behind him are the Battery vehicles, the self-propelled vehicle and the L6/40 ammunition cart. Author colouring.

▼ A self-propelled 105/25 (StuG M43) well camouflaged and abandoned by its servants in an area near Neptune is inspected by Allied soldiers. Author colouring.

OPERATIONAL USE

■ **OPERATIONAL CAMPAIGNS** (*of all self-propelled vehicles*)

The forces of the Regio Esercito, due to the dramatic period the Italian armed forces went through during 1943, received a very small number of self-propelled 75/34 of the 280 planned. Of the divisions that were destined to receive them, at least one self-propelled unit was reported for the Cavalry Regiment 'Cavalleggeri di Alessandria'. The Ariete Armoured Cavalry Division, formed on 1 April 1943, and its CXXXV Battalion Semoventi Controcarri, received fewer than 20 self-propelled vehicles. With these few forces, the Division, now renamed 135th D.C Ariete II, was ordered in September to contribute to the defence of Rome by Marshal Badoglio, with its armoured battalion stationed in the area of the Roman Castles at Cesano. However, the unit, placed north of Rome, ended up surrendering to the former Allies on 10 September.

The 75/46, on the other hand, had an operational life that is little known today, as it operated mainly with German forces. It is known that it was part of plans for units made up of German Panzerjäger squadrons and German-equipped Italian tank fighters. Then it was certainly used by some Germanic formations whose possible equipment has only been speculated upon, such as the 26th panzer division, or the 148th infantry division as part of its armoured units.

The 105/25 'Dachshund' was also produced in low numbers before September 43. Of these, 12 were used in 1943 by the 135th Armoured Division 'Aries II', which clashed with German troops near Rome in the days following the Italian government's Armistice, on 8 and 9 September 1943, and gave an excellent performance. These are the main facts. Immediately after the Armistice, the German command, which had long foreseen the Italian defection, launched *Fall Achse* (Operation Axis), intended to dismantle the entire Royal Italian Army. On 9 September 1943, the morning after the radio announcement of the Armistice, the 135ª Armoured Division engaged German troops in the town of Cesano and on the Via Ostiense leading to Rome. It is still very difficult to establish in which part of Rome these units took part in the fighting, as the Armoured Division fought in many quarters of Rome, such as those in support of the 21st Infantry Division 'Granatieri di Sardegna' at Porta San Paolo, or with members of the Italian Africa Police and the 18th Bersaglieri Regiment near the Colosseum.

During all the fighting, four M43 Semoventi da 105/25 of the DCI° Gruppo Corazzato were destroyed. It is unclear whether they were all destroyed by German weapons or whether some were sabotaged by the crews before escaping and in some cases joining the Italian partisan resistance. For the record, the German operation known as *Fall Achse* lasted until 19 September 1943 and resulted in the death of over 20,000 Italian soldiers, the capture of over a million Italian soldiers, almost 3,500 anti-tank or anti-aircraft guns, howitzers or field guns, 16,600 trucks or cars and about a thousand armoured or armoured vehicles. A real debacle that gives an idea of the great confusion and disorganisation of the Italian army and especially its leadership in those days. Among the many captured armoured vehicles were the 26 surviving M43 Semoventi M43 mit 105/25, which were later renamed *Beutepanzer Sturmgeschütz* M43 mit 105/25 853(i). For the duration of the war, the Germans had another 91 StuG M43 mit 105/25 853(i) produced after the armistice. This meant that the Wehrmacht used a total of 116 M43 mit 105/25. The Germans themselves, who considered the self-propelled 105/25s to be excellent vehicles, employed them effectively against the Anglo-American forces. The 90/53 self-propelled gun was planned to serve on the Eastern Front. And the planned groups using the thirty available were organised in the spring of 1942. Departure for Russia was planned for October of the same year.

However, at the last moment, the destination changed and the vehicles had to reach Sicily for the defence of the island. Here the vehicles arrived in December of the same year. They had their baptism of fire during the Allied landings in July 1943. On the Licata front, they lost three self-propelled vehicles in the fighting.

On 17 July, only a few self-propelled vehicles remained useful. In the end, none of the armoured vehicles were able to be transported to the continent and thus all the equipment was lost in battle or captured. This was also the last time these vehicles went into battle with Italian forces. After the armistice, some pieces left in Nettuno were instead used by the Germans. They christened the vehicles Beute Gepanzerte-Selbstfahrlafette 9.0 cm KwK L/53 801(i) and assigned them to the Stabskompanie of the Panzer-Regiment of the 26ª Panzer Division. Only one vehicle was deployed by the unit in the Chieti area.

IN THE SERVICE OF THE ITALIAN SOCIAL REPUBLIC

After the armistice, Benito Mussolini was freed by the Germans from his imprisonment on the Gran Sasso. Under German pressure, a new state was then immediately created in the Italian territories not yet under Allied control, the German-allied Italian Social Republic. This was essentially a puppet state under German control. Some of the new vehicles lost from the control of the royal army competed in the republican army, few in truth since the Germans took them all for themselves. A 75/34 was assigned to the 'San Giusto' Armoured Squadron Group. However, it remained in repair for the remainder of the conflict. The other armoured unit, the Leonessa framed in the GNR, was assigned 24 75/34 self-propelled vehicles on paper. In reality, it seems that none of these vehicles ever reached the unit, which was assigned to some German Panzerjäger-Abteilung operating in Italy. At the turn of 1944-45, a 105/25 Bassotto was also used by the RSI's 'Leoncello' Armoured Group near Brescia.

PARTISAN SEMOVENTI

In the hectic days of the end of the conflict, some vehicles passed into the hands of partisan formations. The first of these vehicles, a 75/34, was found by partisans still in the workshop in Turin, together with two M14/42 tanks, participating in a truly surrealist battle against Nazi-Fascist forces inside the workshop. A 75/46 had a similar fate, not in Turin but in Milan: the partisans took possession of a vehicle found abandoned at the workshops of the Milanese steel foundry, Fonderia Milanese di Acciaio Vanzetti SA.

▲ The 75/34 captured and then taken on 'parade' in Turin by the partisans. (Photo: Paolo Crippa archive).

CAMOUFLAGE AND DISTINGUISH MARKS

The background colours of Italian self-propelled vehicles from their creation until 1945, (the operational period of this use is indicated in brackets) also used for all armoured vehicles, were: R.E. grey green (1936-1945), dark chocolate (1936-1941), reddish brown (1936-1943), ochre (for prototypes), sand (1941-1945), dark sand (1943-1945), dark grey (1941-1943). For camouflage, medium green (1936-1943) and dark red (for prototypes) were used. Medium tanks had not yet been created at the time of the Ethiopian War 1935-1936 and the Spanish Civil War 1937-1939.

National territory 1936-1940 - substantial prevalence of grey-green.

Occupation of Albania and the French Front 1939-1940 - grey green.

Campaign in Greece and Yugoslavia 1940-1941 - grey-green possibly camouflaged with green and sand-coloured specks.

East Africa 1940-1941 - grey green or in the old Ethiopian campaign camouflage reddish brown with green spots.

North Africa 1940-1943 - at first only grey-green, the colour in which they were generally disembarked at destination ports, then sand colour in various variegated versions. Not used in the Russian Campaign 1941-1943.

RSI 1943-1945 - green-grey, dark sand yellow, reddish brown with medium dense green speckling, in uniform German panzer grey colour. In particular, the 'Leonessa' and 'San Giusto' tanks were dark sand-coloured. I also report the presence of elaborate camouflage in irregular chequered patterns with a sandy yellow background and green and brown patches.

BADGES OF SEMOVENTI

In order to recognise individual armoured vehicles in military operations, even for Italy, it became necessary to introduce an identification system, also because at least initially there were no tanks with radio equipment installed. In fact, radios only began to be installed with some regularity from 1941 onwards. In the beginning, flags with red or white drapes were used for communication. The first table of distinctive tank markings dates back to 1925 and was very complex and articulated, to the point of excess. Number groups were not introduced until 1927, after the establishment of the Tank Regiment; new regulations were issued in 1928.

These official tables never mentioned the markings for **self-propelled vehicles.** It so happened that many units followed their directives, while others went their own way. Thus the most disparate symbols appeared on the hulls, from the black tortoise of the ram division to the centaur with a bow on horseback for the division of the same name. Colourful geometric figures (circles, triangles or rhombuses) of various sizes were used. Soon, however, the use of triangles (typical of self-propelled vehicles only) became standardised, at least in the 'Ariete'.

These were triangles with the tip pointing downwards, and inverted in the case of command tanks. They were either single-coloured or two-coloured in the colour choices already adopted for the tanks: the first battery had red, 2ª blue, 3ª yellow, 4ª green; white was reserved for the command tanks. The first batteries had a single-coloured triangle. The triangles of the various batteries were surmounted by an Arabic number (of the colour of the battery) indicating the self-propelled unit in the organic formation of the department.

Some of the self-propelled units adopted coloured guidons on the radio antennas, the same colour for each group: for example, the DLIV group had red cloth guidons with a different central yellow geometric design for each of the twelve self-propelled units in the division. These symbols, for this group belonging to the Littorio Division, were also painted, again in red, on the rear bulkhead of the casemate.

The self-propelled vehicles of the CCXXX Assault Group operating in Sicily in 1943, instead of the triangle, used as a badge a sort of black guidon, also triangular, with the effigy of a skull resting on white crossbones. Each vehicle could also be distinguished by a precise designation written in white on a rectangle on a red background on the side of the hull, which also served as an identification code for radio calls.

The first battery of the DLVII group, for example, chose the names of the great Italian condottieri of the Renaissance: Fieramosca, Biancamano, Malatesta, Carmagnola, Montecuccoli, Colleoni and Fortebraccio, while the self-propelled vehicles of the 2ª battery used the names of ancient weapons: Arrow, Sling, Strale, Picca, Dardo and Alabarda.

Other groups adopted the name of old rifles and artillery such as: Archibugio, Spingarda, Colubruna, etc. A number of self-propelled vehicles, in honour of the fact that they belonged to the artillery, bore the armoured artillery emblem (crossed cannons surmounted by a grenade and horizontal flame) painted on the front right side of the casemate (as a rule, it was on the left side). In time, however, they increasingly saw the use of the coloured rectangles already in use on medium and light tanks. The self-propelled batteries were represented by coloured rectangles in the manner already indicated for triangles.

As a sign of aerial identification, a white Savoy cross was sometimes painted on the vehicles, placed, depending on the type of vehicle, on the turret or engine compartment ceiling.

As of 1941, a white disc of about 70 cm in diameter was painted instead of the cross. Despite circulars and instructions as already mentioned, there were numerous exceptions and variations to the official regulations. The self-propelled vehicles that later passed into the hands of the Italian Social Republic showed the distinctive signs of the various departments painted on them: the 'Leonessa' had a slightly more complicated distinguishing sign formed by the red M of Mussolini, cut by a black bundle and underneath the inscription, also in black, 'GNR'.

The 'San Giusto' Armoured Squadron Group adopted a symbol consisting of a simple tricolour, to which the silhouette of a black tank was added from the spring of 1944. The tricolour was later (autumn 1944) replaced with a waving one and the silhouette of the tank with that of a self-propelled vehicle. The self-propelled vehicles captured and later reused by the Germans, (and in addition to these also the new ones ordered after the armistice of 1944) bore the typical German army markings starting with the black and white *ritterkreuz* in its various shapes. The same applied to the camouflage, with 'German' colours for the vehicles that had become part of the German arm.

▲ M13/40 and 75/34 self-propelled tank of the 'San Giusto' during an exercise in the countryside at the end of 1944, both with the new camouflage colouring, (Photo: Paolo Crippa archive). Author colouring.

▲ The 75/34 self-propelled vehicle is prepared to receive camouflage colouring. Paolo Crippa Archive.

▼ Interesting picture showing the crew of a 90/53 self-propelled vehicle in full, intent on loading the piece. Note also the ammunition carrier made from the L6/40's hull, equipped among other things with a Breda machine gun for close-range defence. Crippa archive. Author's colouring.

BIBLIOGRAPHY

- Nicola Pignato *I mezzi blindo-corazzati italiani 1923-1943*, Storia Militare, 2005.
- Paolo Crippa *Storia dei reparti corazzati della Repubblica Sociale Italiana 1943/1945*, Marvia Edizioni, 2006.
- Pafi, Falessi, Fiore, *Corazzati Italiani 1939-1945*, D'Anna Editore, Roma, 1968. ISBN non esistente
- Nicola Pignato e Filippo Cappellano *Gli Autoveicoli da Combattimento dell'Esercito Italiano*, Volume Secondo, Tomo II – Ufficio Storico dello Stato Maggiore dell'Esercito – 2002
- Filippo Cappellano e Pier Paolo Battistelli *Carri armati medi italiani 1939-45*; New Vanguard Book 195 – Osprey Publishing, 20 dicembre 2012
- Antonio Tallillo, Andrea Tallillo e Daniele Guglielmi *Carro M – Carri Medi M11/39, M13/40, M14/41, M15/42, Semoventi ed Altri Derivati Volume Primo e Secondo* - Gruppo Modellistico Trentino di Studio e Ricerca Storica, 2012
- Nicola Pignato e Filippo Cappellano *Andare contro i carri armati. L'evoluzione della difesa controcarro nell'esercito italiano dal 1918 al 1945* – Udine 2008
- Ralph A. Riccio *Carri armati italiani e veicoli da combattimento della Seconda Guerra Mondiale* – Mattioli 1885 – 2010
- Giulio Benussi *Semicingolati, Motoveicoli e Veicoli Speciali del Regio Esercito Italiano 1919-1943* –Edizioni Intergest – 1976.
- *Semoventi M41 & M42*. Daniele Guglielmi. Armor Photogallery -Broncos (in inglese).
- Janusz Ledwoch *Tank Power vol. CLXXXIII 443. Semovente da 75/32-34-46, 90/53, 105/25* - Polonia Widawnictwo militaria.
- Luca Stefano Cristini *Italian Medium tank M13/40, M14/41 & M15/42* - Luca Stefano Cristini serie TEW Soldiershop. Italia 2022.
- Luca Stefano Cristini *Semovente 75/18 e 75/34* - Luca Stefano Cristini serie TEW Soldiershop. Italia 2021.
- Luca Stefano Cristini *I carri leggeri CV3 L-33-35-38* - Luca Stefano Cristini serie TEW Soldiershop. Italia 2022.
- Luca Stefano Cristini *Carro leggero italiano L6-40 e Semovente L40* - Luca Stefano Cristini serie TEW Soldiershop. Italia 2023.
- Lorenzo Bovi, Antonio e Andrea Talillo. *Semoventi da 47/32, 90/53 e 75/18 in Sicilia*. Ediz. illustrata - Ardite edizioni 2021. Italia
- Paolo Crippa e Carlo Cucut *I reparti corazzati italiani nei Balcani*, Soldiershop 2019
- Paolo Crippa *I reparti corazzati del R.E. E l'armistizio 1° Volume*, Soldiershop 2021.
- Paolo Crippa *I reparti corazzati del R.E. E l'armistizio 2° Volume*, Soldiershop 2021.Paolo Crippa *Il gruppo corazzato del Leoncello*, Soldiershop 2021.
- Ugo Barlozzetti e A. Pirella *Mezzi dell'Esercito Italiano 1935-45*, Editoriale Olimpia, 1986.
- *Panzer tracts No. 19-2 Beute Panzerkampfwagen, carri armati britannici, americani, russi e italiani catturati dal 1940 al 1945* – Thomas L. Jentz e W. Regenberg – Panzer Tracts – 2008
- *Mussolini Tanks - Tank Powwer vol. XXIX*. Polonia Widawnictwo militaria.
- *Corazzati e blindati italiani dalle origini allo scoppio della seconda guerra mondiale*, David Vannucci, Editrice Innocenti, 2003.

TITLES ALREADY PUBLISHED
ALL BOOKS IN THE SERIES ARE PRINTED IN ITALIAN OR IN ENGLISH

VISIT OUR WEBSITE FOR MORE INFORMATION ON
THE WEAPONS ENCYCLOPAEDIA:
https://soldiershop.com/collane/libri/the-weapons-encyclopaedia/

TWE-020 EN

www.ingramcontent.com/pod-product-compliance
Lightning Source LLC
LaVergne TN
LVHW070523070526
838199LV00072B/6690

9791255890782